TEN WAYS TO STUDY YOUR BIBLE

09/20/16

John 3:16
Romans 5:1

BRUCE LACKEY

©1983, Bruce P. Lackey

Printed in Canada
By Bethel Baptist Print Ministry
4212 Campbell St. N.
London, Ontario
N6P 1A6

(866) 295-4143 (toll Free)
www.bethelbaptist.ca (website)
info@bethelbaptist.ca (e-mail)

Ten Ways to Study Your Bible

Table Of Contents

Introduction

INTRODUCTION

These materials have been gleaned from much interest and research regarding the various methods of Bible study, beginning with a college course which the author took many years ago and continuing through years of teaching and pastoring. Many books on the subject have been read, and while none of them has been copied, it would have been impossible not to have been influenced by them.

This book is the result of, not only those many books, but also actual techniques hammered out on the anvil of personal study for Bible classes and preaching services. They are tried and proven. Also, many students have testified to the profit of learning and using these methods.

May the Spirit of God, who moved men to write the holy scriptures, use these chapters to the edifying of God's people everywhere.

Chapter 1

Basic Tools For Bible Study

1. A good, complete concordance which gives the meaning of the words in Hebrew and Greek, such as:

   Strong's Exhaustive Concordance, by James Strong (various publishers)

   Young's Analytical Concordance, by Robert Young (Eerdmans)

2. The Treasury of Scripture Knowledge, with introduction by R.A. Torrey, published by Fleming H. Revell Company. This book gives parallel references to every verse in the Bible, with a total of approximately five hundred thousand.

3. A Bible with references on each page and any of the following: footnotes, chain references, topical indexes, introductions to the books of the Bible. Examples are the Scofield Reference Bible and Thompson Chain Reference Bible.

4. A Bible handbook (such as Unger's or Halley's) or a one-volume commentary (preferably one which uses many authors. Wycliffe, published by Moody Press, is a good one).

5. A Bible dictionary or a Bible encyclopedia.

FOR THE STUDENT WHO KNOWS GREEK

1. Greek New Testament. This author recommends the Textus Receptus, from which the King James Version was translated. It may be obtained from the Trinitarian Bible Society, 26 Gracey Blvd.,

Weston, Ontario, Canada, M9R 1Z9. The Stephens text of 1550 is substantially the same. It is published by Zondervan in an interlinear form.

2. The Englishman's Greek Concordance, various publishers. Some are number-keyed to Strong's Concordance.

3. An analytical Greek lexicon.

4. Thayer's Greek-English Lexicon, by Joseph Henry Thayer, various publishers.

5. Synonyms of the New Testament, R. C. Trench, Eerdmans.

6. The Vocabulary Of The Greek Testament, by Moulton and Milligan, Eerdmans. Helpful in showing the meaning of the words of the New Testament as they were used in the secular literature of the day.

7. A Manual Grammar Of The Greek New Testament, by Dana and Mantey, MacMillan.

Chapter 2

The Spiritual Requirements For Bible Study

The requirements for learning the Bible are primarily spiritual, not intellectual. Therefore, it is not a lack of formal education or intellectual accomplishment that hinders our knowledge of God's Word, but the lack of one or more of the following:

The first requirement is that one must be saved. But the natural man receiveth not the things of the Spirit of God: for they are foolishness unto him: neither can he know them, because they are spiritually discerned, (I Cor. 2:14). The natural man is one who has had only a natural birth; he has not had the supernatural birth which the Lord Jesus required in John 3:7, when He said, *Ye must be born again.* The word *natural* is used in I Corinthians 15:44 and 46 to describe the physical body, in contrast to the spiritual body. This usage gives us a further insight to the natural man: he is governed by his natural body. Many people think that a human being is nothing more than a body; they think that the mind is the brain, so that if the brain is physically altered, the mind is affected. Such is the reasoning of *the natural man.* Ephesians 2:3 teaches that, before we are saved, we live to satisfy the desires of this body. Living such a life hinders one from knowing God's Word, because it is spiritually discerned.

Even though the natural man might learn some verses from scripture, he can not know by experience what it means to be fed by the Word, or strengthened by the Spirit, or be assured of salvation, since not a single one of these things is experienced through the body.

If a person is having trouble understanding the Bible, the first thing he should do is examine his heart in the light of the Bible to see whether he is saved. Some of the evidences of salvation are:

(1) Obedience to scripture (I Jn 2:3-5)

(2) Love for God's children (I Jn. 3:14)

(3) Overcoming the world (I Jn. 5:4)

(4) Becoming a new creature, with old things passing away and all things becoming new (II Cor. 5:17)

(5) Hearing the voice of Christ and following Him (Jn. 10:27)

If one finds that he does not have these Biblical evidences, he should repent of his rebellion against God, believe that Christ died for his sins and rose again, and receive the Lord Jesus as his personal Savior. Scriptures which teach the way of salvation are:

(1) Isaiah 53:6, *All we like sheep have gone astray; we have turned every one to his own way; and the Lord hath laid on him the iniquity of us all.*

(2) I Corinthians 15:3-4, *Christ died for our sins according to the scriptures; and that he was buried, and that he rose again the third day according to the scriptures.*

(3) John 1:12, *But as many as received him, to them gave he power to become the sons of God, even to them that believe on his name.*

Once that issue is settled, he can go on to the other

spiritual qualifications.

The second requirement is that one must not be carnal, because the carnal Christian *is not able to bear* the meat of the Word (I Cor. 3:1-4). These *babes in Christ* have the characteristics of a baby: selfishness, idleness, and unconcern for cleanliness. As a result, they envy others, stir up strife, and cause divisions among believers, and must have milk rather than meat.

God's use of these two kinds of food as symbols of His truth is very enlightening. Since both milk and meat could come from the same animal, they would be essentially the same, nutritionally. The difference is that milk is pre-digested, and is suitable for babies whose digestive systems have not fully developed. The carnal Christian can not digest the Word himself because he is so occupied with himself and his envy of others, with the resultant strife and divisions, that he has no time or desire for the study, prayer, and obedience that are necessary for growing and digesting the scriptures. Thus, someone must do it for him and spoon-feed him the milk of the Word. Carnal Christians must remedy the selfishness problem with Luke 9:23 and the envy-strife-divisions problem with Luke 12:15 and Romans 12:10. Then, they will be able not only to *bear* the meat of the scripture, but enjoy it as well.

The third requirement is to use what we learn, as shown by Hebrews 5:14, *But strong meat belongeth to them that are of full age, even to those who by reason of use have their senses exercised to discern both good and evil.* The word *use* means a habitual use. We must practice what we learn from scripture, if we would discern the meat of the Word. Thus, the Bible speaks of repeated times of prayer (Ps. 55:17); regular worship

(Lk. 4:16); weekly giving (I Cor. 16:2). As we practice, we grow; spiritual obedience is spiritual exercise, enabling us to discern between good and evil interpretations of scripture.

The fourth requirement is to have faith. Hebrews 11:3 enunciates the principle when it says, *Through faith we understand that the worlds were framed by the word of God.* Creation is a definite teaching of scripture and must be understood by faith, since it cannot be proved by scientific observation. This principle would apply to every truth of God's Word: first we must believe it; then we will be able to understand it. We use this principle many times in everyday life: we believe the power of electricity and enjoy the benefits of it, but most of us do not understand how it works. The same is true of our use of doctors, pharmacists, automobiles, etc. Likewise, and even more so, we must believe God's Word about the clear doctrines of the trinity, inspiration, etc., even though we do not understand how it all happened. The same would be true of problem passages, such as the numerical differences in the Books of Kings and Chronicles, as well as other difficult verses. God's first requirement is that we believe Him and that necessarily includes believing His Word. If there is unquestioning faith, we may expect understanding to follow, in God's good time, as we obey Him.

The fifth requirement is discipline and stability. II Peter 3:16 speaks of a common problem when it tells of those who are unlearned and unstable wresting the scriptures to their own destruction. The word *unlearned* means to be undisciplined, having no regularity or self-control. And this type of person is also unstable, that is,

11

unreliable and inconsistent. Proverbs 24:21-22 warns us to *meddle not with them that are given to change: for their calamity shall rise suddenly.* If we would avoid twisting the scriptures to our own destruction, we must learn self-discipline and stability. A review of the remarks made in the third requirement (Heb. 5:14) and obedience to them would go a long way in establishing these characteristics in the Christian's life.

John 7:17 gives the sixth requirement: we must do God's will, if we would know His doctrine. When Christ said, *If any man will . . .* He was emphasizing that the person must have the desire. Doing God's will is not automatic; hence, Colossians 3:1-2 teaches us to *set our affection on . . . seek* things which are above. We must determine to do these things. Of course, God knows whether the desire is genuine or not; if it is, it will produce the actual thing. Therefore, as we apply this verse to Bible study, we must approach scripture with this attitude: "Lord, I want to study your Word so that I can obey you. I desire to know this book so that I can do what you want me to do." When God sees such an attitude of heart, He will certainly teach us His truth. On the other hand, if we want to study the Bible merely to satisfy some idle curiosity, or to win an argument, or to establish a reputation, we will succeed only in wrongly interpreting it. God's book was not given for any of these reasons.

Requirement number seven is implied in Romans 11:33, that is, we must recognize human limitations. *O the depth of the riches both of the wisdom and knowledge of God! How unsearchable are his judgments, and his ways past finding out!* And it is wise to remember that this statement was made at the end of a three-chapter discussion of the doctrine of election. Some of the truths of God are so large in scope that we can not comprehend them fully because we are incapable of doing so. We must not be discouraged by the fact that some biblical truths will always be just beyond our reach, intellectually. Such doctrines as election, the trinity, and the incarnation of Christ have caused much controversy through the centuries, mainly because we refuse to admit that we can not fully explain them. Just as one can not pour the ocean into a quart jar, so we cannot comprehend God in our finite minds. We must believe the Word, understand what we are capable of, and then realize our human limitations.

I John 2:27 reveals the eighth requirement: that of being taught by the Holy Spirit. Luke 4:18 and Acts 10:38 both speak of Christ as being anointed with the Spirit of God. Then, I John 3:24 and 4:13 teach that all believers have the Holy Spirit; thus we conclude that the anointing is the Spirit. This verse does not teach that we have no need of human teachers, since Ephesians 4:12 and I Corinthians 12:28 show that God has given some people the ability to teach in the church. The meaning, according to the context, is that they did not need to subject themselves to those teachers who were outside the church, having left the believers (:19). Since all believers are priests (I Pet. 2:9), we do not have to become slavish disciples to any man or group of men. We are to listen to teachers who teach God's Word and test what they say by scripture. This is the obvious meaning of I Thessalonians 5:20-21, *Despise not prophesyings. Prove all things; hold fast that which is good.* The Holy Spirit will use men to teach us, but it will always be through words which He has given in scripture (I Cor. 2:13). This will be seen by putting I

John 2:27 together with verse 24. Verse 27 says that if the anointing teaches us, we shall abide in Christ. Verse 24 says that if that which we have heard from the beginning remains in us, we shall continue in the Son. Therefore, the Holy Spirit teaches us through the Word, which we heard at the beginning.

As we listen to Bible teachers, read their books, and consider the scriptures, let us have the attitude of dependence on the Spirit of God to enlighten us and open the eyes of our understanding (Eph. 1:17-18).

The last requirement is found in Hosea 6:3, *Then shall we know, if we follow on to know the Lord.* To follow on is to be persistent. If we persist in the foregoing requirements, we can confidently expect to know God's Word. God's choicest servants have learned the value of persistence. Shortly before she was killed by an opium addict, Lillian Hamer, a missionary in Thailand, penned these words:

> My hand is on the plow, my faltering hand;
> But all in front of me is untilled land.
> The wilderness and the solitary place,
> The lonely desert with its interspace.
> What harvest have I, but this paltry grain,
> These dwindling husks, a handful of dry corn,
> These poor lean stalks? My courage is outworn;
> Keep me from turning back.
> The handles of my plow with tears are wet;
> The shears with rust are spoiled, and yet—and yet,
> My God! My God! KEEP ME FROM TURNING BACK.

Chapter 3

How To Study A Book

1. Read the entire book at least ten times, preferably in an unmarked Bible with large print. This will avoid distractions. To begin with, it would be wise to choose a shorter book.

2. Separate the scriptures into paragraphs, then give each one a title. This may be done by noting the paragraph marks which may be in your Bible, or you could make your own paragraph divisions by doing the following: (1) Look for obvious changes of subject. For instance, most of the people in Hebrews 11 take up only one verse, but Abraham and Sarah are discussed in verses 8-19; Moses and his parents, in verses 23-29. (2) Look for words which indicate a change, such as *therefore . . . wherefore . . . now . . . dearly beloved . . . likewise . . . finally . . . forasmuch.* These usually indicate a new paragraph, although there would be exceptions. (3) Compare your paragraphs with those in a study Bible, such as Scofield and Thompson. If you have trouble, see the example beginning on page 19.

3. List the repeated words or phrases, and the references where they are found.

4. List what is taught about each person of the Trinity, and the references for each.

5. List the information which is given about the author, and the references. This would include not only his name, but his circumstances (such as being in prison), his plans, etc.

6. List the information which is given about those to whom the book was written, and the references.

7. List any information which would indicate the date of the book, and the references. Many times this will be information that is very general, but it would still be worth noting.

8. List the information which is given about why the book may have been written, and the references.

9. Determine the main theme(s) of the book. There might be more than one, but never more than three or four.

10. Make a simple outline of the book. Some helpful hints about outlining:

    A. Use the paragraphs which you determined under point 2.
    B. Do not have too many points in the book.
    C. Keep your phrases consistent. That is, do not have:
      I. The Writer
      II. Those to Whom Written
    But, rather:
      I. The Writer
      II. The Recipients
    (or)
      I. The One Who Wrote
      II. Those To Whom Written
    D. Sub-points should not repeat the main point, such as:
      I. Grace
        a. Grace
        b. Mercy
        c. Peace
    In this instance, either the main point should be

changed from *Grace* to something else, or the sub-point *a. Grace* should be eliminated.

E. The main point should describe the whole section; the sub-points should describe each paragraph within the section. Sub-sub-points would be sentences within the paragraph. See the example, beginning on page 25.

EXAMPLE OF THE BOOK METHOD

1. The epistle of I Peter has been read at least ten times.

2. The paragraphs:

1:1-2, Introduction

1:3-12, Praise for God's blessing upon us

1:13-25, Exhortations to holiness

2:1-10, Relationships to God

2:11-25, Relationships to unbelievers

3:1-7, Marital relationships

3:8-12, Attitudes toward evil

3:13 - 4:19, Attitudes toward suffering for righteousness' sake

5:1-4, Instructions to elders

5:5-9, General exhortations

5:10-14, Closing remarks

3. Repeated words and phrases:

(1). Grace, 8 times, 1:2, 10, 13, 3:7, 4:10, 5:5, 10, 12.

(2). Faith, 9 times. 1:5, 7, 8, 9, 21; 2:7, 6, 5:9

(3). Salvation, 6 times 1:5, 9, 10, 20; 3:21; 4:18.

(4). Suffering, 15 times. 1:11; 2:19, 20, 21, 23; 3:14, 17, 18; 4:1, 13, 15, 16, 19; 5:1, 10.

(5). Glory, 12 times. 1:7, 8, 11, 21, 24; 2:20; 4:13, 14; 5:1, 4, 10, 11.

(6). Love, 6 times. 1:8, 22; 2:17; 3:8, 10.

(7). Soul, 6 times. 2:11, 25; 1:9, 22; 3:20; 4:19.

(8). Joy, rejoice, 5 times, 1:6, 8: 4:13.

4.   The teachings about each person   of the Trinity:

(1). The Father

1:2, His foreknowledge is the basis of election.

1:3, He has begotten us again according to His abundant mercy.

1:5, He keeps us by His power through faith.

1:15, He has called us, and is holy.

1:17, He judges according to every man's work, without respect of persons.

1:21, He is the object of our faith and hope.

1:23, His Word produces the new birth and is incorruptible.

1:25, His Word endures forever.

2:3, He is gracious.

2:4, He chose us.

2:5, He accepts us by Jesus Christ.

2:9, He called us from darkness to light. Compare 5:10.

2:10, He has people.

2:12, He will visit.

2:15, He wills that we be law-abiding.

2:17, He is to be feared.

2:20, He accepts our suffering when it is wrongful.

3:4, He considers a meek and quiet spirit to be of

18

great price.

3:12, He sees the righteous, hears their prayers, and is against evil doers.

3:15, He is to be sanctified in our hearts.

3:17, He wills that some suffer for well-doing. Compare 4:19.

4:11, He gives various abilities to His servants through Christ and is to be glorified in our service.

4:17, He has a house. Compare 2:5, 10 (a people), 5:2 (a flock), and 5:3 (a heritage).

4:19, He is the faithful Creator.

5:5, He resists the proud; gives grace to the humble.

5;6, He has a mighty hand.

5:7, He cares for you.

5:10, He is the God of all grace; has called us to His eternal glory by Jesus Christ; will make you perfect, stablish, strengthen, and settle you.

5:11, He is to receive glory and dominion for ever and ever.

(2) The Son

1:2, His blood is sprinkled.

1:3, He was resurrected.

1:7, He will appear.

1:13, He will be revealed.

1:19, His blood redeemed us; is precious; He is a lamb without blemish or spot.

1:20, He was foreordained before the foundation of the world; was manifest in these last times.

1:21, He enables us to believe in God.

2:6, He is the chief cornerstone, elect, precious; was laid by God.

2:7, He is precious to believers; was disallowed; is the head stone of the corner.

2:8, He is a stone of stumbling and a rock of offence.

2:21, He suffered for us, compare 4:1. He left us an example.

2:22, He did no sin, had no guile in His mouth.

2:23, He reviled not in retaliation, nor threatened when He suffered; committed Himself to the Father.

2:24, He bore our sins in His body on the tree.

2:25, He is the Shepherd and Bishop of our souls.

3:18, He suffered for sins and for the unjust. He was put to death in the flesh.

3:19, He preached to the spirits in prison.

3:22, He has gone into heaven; is on the right hand of God; rules over angels, authorities, and powers.

4:5, He is ready to judge the quick and the dead.

5:4, He is the Chief Shepherd, will give a crown of glory to obedient elders.

(3) The Holy Spirit

1:2, He sanctifies.

1:11, He is called the Spirit of Christ; He signified and testified to the prophets the sufferings of Christ and the glory.

1:12, He enables those who preach the gospel; He was sent down from heaven.

1:22, He enabled us to obey the truth.

3:18, He quickened Christ.

3:19, He was associated with Christ's preaching to the spirits.

4:14, He rests upon those who are reproached for the name of Christ.

5. Information about the author:

1:1, An apostle of Jesus Christ.

1:3, He had been begotten again.

2:11, He loved those to whom he wrote. Compare 4:12.

5:1, He was an elder; did not put himself above them. A witness of the sufferings of Christ; a partaker of the glory that shall be revealed.

5:12, He wrote by Silvanus; that is, he used him as an amanuensis.

5:13, He was the father of Marcus (if John Mark is meant, that would be understood as being his father, spiritually).

6. Information about the recipients of the epistle.

1:1, They were called strangers. Compare 2:11. They were located in Pontus, Galatia, Capadocia, Asia, and Bithynia.

1:2, They were Christians. Compare 1:3, 22-23; 5:12.

1:6, They were in heaviness through manifold temptations. Compare 4:12.

1:8, They had not seen Christ, but were rejoicing in Him.

2:10, They were not a people before their conversion.

21

2:18, Some of them were servants.

3:1, Some had unbelieving husbands.

4:3, They had walked in lasciviousness, lusts, excess of wine, revellings, banquetings, and abominable idolatries before conversion.

4:4, They had changed!

5:1,   They had elders; must have been organized into churches.

5:2-3, They were called the flock of God.

7. There is no information about the date the epistle was written.

8. Reasons why the epistle was written:

1:6-7, To encourage them in their trials. Compare 2:18-25; 3:14-18; 4:1-4, 12-19; 5:10.

1:13-16, To encourage them to be holy.

1:22, To encourage them to love one another. Compare 4:8-9.

2:1-2, To encourage them to learn the Word.

2:11-17, To instruct them in the way to live before unbelievers.

3:1-7, To instruct them regarding marital relationships.

5:1-4, To encourage and instruct the elders.

9. The main theme: to exhort them regarding trials, and to testify to them that they were standing in the true grace of God (5:12).

10. The outline of the epistle.

Chapter One

Introduction, verses 1-2
    verse 1, Peter

verses 1-2, The strangers

I. Salvation (verses 3-9)

   A. Source: God (vs. 3)

   B. Basis: Mercy (vs. 3)

   C. Description: begotten again (vs. 3)

   D. Means: resurrection (vs. 3)

   E. Goal: inheritance (vs. 4)

   F. Power: faith (vs. 5)

   G. Problem: temptation (vs. 6)

   H. Purpose: praise, honour, and glory (vs. 7)

   I. Joy (vs. 8)

   J. End (vs. 9)

II. Scriptures (verses 10-25)

   A. Instruments: prophets (vs. 10)

   B. Content: grace (vs. 10)

   C. Author: the Spirit (vs. 11)

   D. Manner: signify and testify (vs. 11)

   E. Theme: sufferings and glory (vs. 11)

   F. Marvel (vs. 12)

   G. Application (verses 13-23)

   H. Preservation (verses 23-25)

Chapter Two

I Hunger For the Word (verses 1-3)

   A. Because of 1:11 and 23-25

   B. Laying aside all malice, etc. (vs.1)

   C. As newborn babes (vs. 2)

   D. For the Word (vs. 2)

   E. For those who have tasted (vs. 3)

II House Of God (verses 4-10)

   A. Those who have come to the miraculous one

(vs. 4)
    B. Those who are miraculous also (vs. 5)
    C. For God to dwell in (vs. 5)
    D. To offer spiritual sacrifices (vs. 5)
    E. Built on the chief corner stone (verses 6-8)
    F. A chosen generation, etc. (verses 9-10)
III   Honesty Of Life (verses 11-25)
    A. Toward everyone (verses 11-12)
    B. Toward the government (verses13-17)
    C. Toward supervisors (verses 18-25)

Chapter Three

I. The Home (verses 1-7)
    A. Wives (verses 1-6)
    B. Husbands (vs. 7)
II. The Church (verses 8-12)
    A. Unity (verses 8-12)
    B. Compassion (verses 8-9)
    C. Results (verses 10-12)
III. The World (verses 13-22)
    A. Possibility of suffering (verses 13-14)
    B. Reaction (verses 15-16)
    C. Reason for suffering (vs. 17)
    D. Example of suffering (verses 18-22)

Chapter Four

I. The Will of God Regarding Sanctification (verses 1-6)
    A. Right thinking (verses 1-2)
    B. Contrast (verses 2-5)
    C. Suffering (vs. 6)

II. The Will of God Regarding Service (verses 7-11)
  A. Because the end is at hand (vs. 7)
  B. Have fervent charity (vs. 8)
  C. Use hospitality (vs. 9)
  D. According to your gift (verses 10-11)
III. The Will of God Regarding Suffering (verses 12-19)
  A. Think it not strange (vs. 12)
  B. It brings joy at the second coming (vs. 13)
  C. It causes the Spirit to rest upon us (vs. 14)
  D. It must be undeserved (vs. 15)
  E. It glorifies God (vs. 16)
  F. It is all during this life (vs. 17)
  G. It shows the lost what he must face (vs. 18)
  H. We should commit ourselves to the Creator (vs. 19)

Chapter Five

I. Duties Of An Elder (verses 1-4)
  A. Be exhorted (vs. 1)
  B. Feed (vs. 2)
  C. Take the oversight (verses 2-3)
  D. Expect the reward (vs. 4)
II. Duties Of All Christians (verses 5-9)
  A. Be subject to the elder (vs. 5)
  B. Be clothed with humility (verses 5-6)
  C. Cast all your care upon Him (vs. 7)
  D. Be sober (vs. 8)
  E. Watch for Satan (vs. 8)
  F. Resist Satan (vs. 9)

III God's Great Climax (verses 10-11)
   Closing Remarks (verses 12-14)

Chapter 4

How To Study A Chapter

1. Read the chapter at least ten times, without stopping to make notes or look up parallel verses. Try to read it in one sitting, or at least two or three times in one sitting.

2. Determine the main thought or thoughts. For example, the main thought of Hebrews 11 is faith; that of I Corinthians 13 is charity; I Thessalonians 4 has two: sanctification (verses 1-12) and the second coming of Christ (verses 13-18).

3. List the verses which have the greatest appeal to you, either as an encouragement, a revelation, or a rebuke.

4. List the persons who are named, or the types of persons who are mentioned, and write the information which is given about each.

5. If there are any commands, list them.

6. If there are any promises, list them.

7. If there are any lessons, list them.

8. List significant words which are repeated and the verses in which they are found.

9. Define any words which are unfamiliar to you. Use Strong's Concordance or an English dictionary which has obsolete or archaic or Old English meanings. Page 37 tells how to use Strong's Concordance to define a word.

10. Determine whether the chapter (1) stands alone, or (2) is a continuation of something that was

begun in the previous chapter, or (3) is an introduction to the following chapter.

11. List what is taught about the Father, the son, and the Holy Spirit, and the verses which teach them.

12. Solve any doctrinal problems, which you may have, regarding any verse in the chapter, by doing the following:

(1) List the obvious teachings of the verse.

(2) Use parallel passages, which may be found in your center reference column in your Bible, or from the Treasury of Scripture Knowledge.

(3) Define words.

(4) Fit the verse into the context.

13. Make a simple outline, based on the information you learned in points 2, 4, 5, 6, 7, 8, or 11.

EXAMPLE OF THE CHAPTER METHOD-

I Thessalonians 3

1. I have read it ten times.

2. Main thought: Paul's concern that the Thessalonians be faithful.

3. Verse 5 shows me that he wanted them not only to be saved, but faithful, consistent Christians. Anything less would have meant that his labor was in vain. Verse 10 tells me that even Christians who have such great characteristics as these Thessalonians (see 1:6 and 8) need much more!

4. The persons mentioned:

(1). Paul is prominent, although he is unnamed.
   a. He sent Timothy to encourage the Thessalonians (:1-5)
   b. He was comforted by Timothy's good report (:6-8)
   c. He prayed for them (:9:10).
   d. He wanted to see them and help them make spiritual progress (:11).
(2). Timotheus
   a. Paul's brother (:2).
   b. Minister of God (:2).
   c. Paul's fellow-laborer (:2).
   d. Sent by Paul to help the Thessalonians (:2)
   e. Brought back an encouraging report (:6).
   f. Shared Paul's comfort regarding the Thessalonians (:7-10).
(3). The Thessalonians are mentioned, but unnamed.
   a. Had faith and charity (:6).
   b. Remembered Paul and Timothy and wanted to see them again.

5. There are no commands.

6. There are no promises.

7. The lessons:
   (1) We are appointed to suffer afflictions (:3-4).
   (2) If the tempter succeeds in tempting us, the original goal of the one who won us to Christ will be defeated (:5).
   (3) Soulwinners should be concerned that their converts follow on with the Lord (:2, 6-8).

(4) Soulwinners should pray for their converts (:10).

(5) We should trust God the Father and the Lord Jesus to direct our ways (:11).

(6) The Lord wants us to increase in love toward one another (:12).

(7) Paul's love for the Thessalonians is our example in loving one another (:12).

(8) Our hearts may be established unblameable in holiness when Christ comes (:13).

8. Repeated words: (1) Comfort, verses 2 and 7; (2) Faith, verses 2, 5, 6, 7, 10; (3) establish, verses 2 and 13.

9. Words which need to be defined: only one: *forbear*, verses 1, 5. It is number 4722 in Strong's Concordance and means to cover with silence or to endure patiently. It is also translated *bear, suffer*.

10. Does the chapter stand alone? No, because the word *wherefore* in verse one connects it to the previous chapter, continuing and expanding the idea of Paul's genuine love for them.

11. The teachings about each person of the Trinity:

(1) God, the Father

a. Has ministers (:2).

b. Is the object of our prayers (:9-10).

c. Directs our ways (:11).

(2) Christ

a. The gospel is His (:2).

b. Directs our ways (:11) along with the Father.

c. Enables us to increase and abound in love

30

toward one another (:13).

    d. Will come again with all His saints (:13), a reference to His return at the end of the tribulation.

  (3) The Holy Spirit is not mentioned.

12. Doctrinal problems which need to be solved: when verse 5 says, *lest by some means the tempter have tempted you, and our labour be in vain,* does it teach that they would lose salvation if they yielded to temptation? This is solved by doing the following:

  (1) Obvious teachings:

    a. Paul wanted to know their faith.

    b. The tempter might have used various means to tempt them.

    c. If they yielded, Paul's labor would have been in vain.

  (2) Parallel passages (from The Treasury Of Scripture Knowledge): I Corinthians 15:10 shows that the phrase *in vain* refers to a life of service. Therefore, we are talking about service, not salvation. Also, II Corinthians 6:1-3 shows that *in vain* refers to living in such a way that we do not give any offense or cause the ministry to be blamed. Again, it is service, not salvation.

  (3) Definition: *vain* is number 2756 in Strong's and is translated *empty* in Mark 12:3. Paul's labor would have been empty if they had not served the Lord, because their works would be burned up at the judgment seat of Christ (I Cor. 3:13-15) and they would be empty of reward, thus leaving an empty spot in His service record. II John 8 shows that we share

in the lives of our converts.

(4) The context shows that Paul was assured of their salvation; he knew that they were God's elect (1:4) and that he would be rejoicing in them at the second coming (2:19). This could hardly be true if they might be lost. Rather, he is concerned about their faith (verses 2, 6, 7, 10), their love (verses 6, 12), and their progress (vs. 12). The issue, then, is not salvation, which is by grace, but their works.

13. Some possible outlines of this chapter:

(1) Based on number 2, the main thought: Paul's concern for them
   1. Sending Timothy (verses 1-5)
   2. Hearing from Timothy (verses 6-8)
   3. Praying for them (verses 9-10)
   4. Wanting to visit them (verses 11-13)

(2) Based on number 4:
   1. Paul's concern (verses 1, 5, 6-13)
   2. Timothy's visit (verses 2, 6)
   3. The Thessalonians' obedience (verses 6-8)

(3) Based on number 7: the outline would be the same as the lessons listed there.

(4) Based on number 8:
   1. Comfort
      a. For the Thessalonians (vs. 2)
      b. For Paul (vs. 7)
   2. Faith
      a. It needed to be comforted (vs. 2)
      b. It was attacked by Satan (vs. 5)

c. It was stedfast (vs. 6)

d. It encouraged Paul (vs. 7)

e. It needed to be perfected (vs. 10)

3. Establish

a. Done by Timothy (vs. 2)

b. Done by Christ (vs. 13)

Chapter 5

How To Study Devotionally

1. Read the passage at least ten times. Great expository preachers of the past would read a book ten, twenty, even fifty times before attempting to expound it. The most important aspect of Bible study is to saturate your mind and heart with the very words of scripture.

2. Define each obscure word. A good English dictionary which gives obsolete or archaic definitions may be helpful, but the best tool would be Strong's Concordance or Young's Concordance. Using Strong's, look up the English word and find the verse which is in your passage; then notice the number to the right. Look up this number in the back of the concordance. If the number is upright, it is in the Hebrew dictionary. If it is slanted, it is in the Greek. After seeing the Hebrew or Greek word, you will see a definition, then a dash. Following the dash will be given all the English words by which the Hebrew or Greek word is translated. Sometimes, noticing all these translations will give you a better definition than anything else. For instance, the word *prevent* in I Thessalonians 4:15 is from #5348, which is translated *(already) attain, come, prevent.* Therefore, we see that the basic meaning is to come before. Using Young's we would learn the definition on the same page as the English word, then we would see that it is from the Greek word *phthano.* Looking on page 85 of the Index-Lexicon in the back of the book, we would see the English translations of this word, and come to the same conclusion; the old meaning of *prevent* is to go before.

3. Solve any doctrinal problem, by (1) writing the obvious teachings of the passage, (2) using parallel passages from your reference Bible or from the Treasury Of Scripture Knowledge, (3) defining words as explained in the previous paragraph, being careful not to forget the synonyms, and (4) fitting the verse into the context.

4. Write the passage in your own words, using the information you gained in #2 & 3. This is not to improve or correct the King James Version, but to see whether you understand it. It is not wrong to put scripture in your own words, or to paraphrase it, when you are doing so to explain it to others or to apply it to your own life. Matthew 4:15-16 is a paraphrase of Isaiah, 9:1-2, giving us an example of the way the Holy Spirit sometimes paraphrased an Old Testament scripture in the New Testament. Of course, we must be careful that we do not change the meaning.

5. Write the passage in the first person. For example, John 3:16 would read, "For God so loved me, that he gave his only begotten Son, that if I would believe in him, I would not perish, but have everlasting life." The purpose of this is to get the personal profit from each verse.

6. Memorize the verse from the passage that speaks to your heart at the time you are studying it.

EXAMPLE OF THE DEVOTIONAL METHOD-

II Corinthians 5:1-10

1. The passage has been read ten times.

2. The only obscure word is *whilst* (:6). It is old English for *while*. This could be learned from an

35

English dictionary.

3. Various problems:

(1) Do verses 1-4 refer to an intermediate body which the Christian will have before the resurrection, or to the resurrection body, or to the heavenly city? Solution:

(a) First, we list what is obviously taught. Verse 1 shows that the house is God's building, it is eternal, in the heavens, and verse 2 says that it is from heaven.

(b) Parallel verses, from the Treasury of Scripture Knowledge. The most significant are John 14:2-3, which describe the mansions that are being prepared for u s by Christ, and Hebrews 11:10, which tells of the city whose builder and maker is God.

(c) Then we define words. The word *house* is #3614 in Strong, where we learn that the Greek word is also translated *home* (Mt. 8:6) and *household* (Phil. 4:22). Since these verses do not help us in interpreting our passage, we confine ourselves to the word *house*. Matthew 7:24 uses it referring to a building, whereas Matthew 12:25 and John 4:53 use it to refer to a family. The synonym *building* refers to the whole body of Christ (I Cor. 3:9; Eph. 2:21) and the temple (Mt. 24:1). The word *house* in verse 2 is translated *habitation* in Jude 6, referring to the location or manner in which the angels lived before they sinned. Also, Peter uses

36

tabernacle to refer to his body (II Pet. 1:13 -14, where the Greek word is the same root used here.)

(d) In the context, there has been a contrast between earthly and heavenly bodies: see II Corinthians 4:7, 10, 14, 16, and 18. Conclusion: although it could refer to the heavenly city, it more likely refers to the resurrection body, because (1) the context has been contrasting earthly and heavenly bodies, and the word *for* (5:1) definitely ties this paragraph to the previous chapter. (2) Peter used the word *tabernacle* similarly. (3) Philippians 3:20-21 and I Corinthians 15:42-49 also contrast the earthly and heavenly bodies. (4) The possibility of being clothed with our heavenly house, yet being naked (:2-3), seems to refer to the fine linen which saints will wear at the marriage of the Lamb. This fine linen reveals the righteous deeds of the saints (Rev. 19:8) rather than the righteousness of Christ. Hence, we have the warning given in Revelation 16:15 to watch and keep our garments, lest we walk naked and others see our shame. (5) The phrase *to be clothed . . .* in verses 2-4 seems to be parallel with I Corinthians 15:53-54 which describes the change from the mortal body to the immortal.

In any case, there is no indication here of an intermediate body which we would receive before the resurrection, mainly because the body discussed here is said to be eternal (:1). The paragraph states that we are confident of two things: we will have a glorified, resurrection body; but even before then, if we are absent from this body, we will be present with the Lord (:8).

> (2) Problem #2: does verse 9 teach the possibility of a Christian's being rejected and cast out of heaven? Solution:
>
> > (a) The passage is too short for listing obvious teachings.
> >
> > (b) Ephesians 1:6 is parallel, showing that we are accepted in the beloved, so that our position is dependent on Him. Hebrews 12:28 tells of the necessity of serving God acceptably.
> >
> > (c) Defining words is most helpful, here. *Labor* is #5389 in Strong and is translated *strive* (Rom. 15:20, describing Paul's preaching) and *study* (I Thes. 4:11, referring to our effort to be quiet and mind our own business.) *Accepted* is #2101, translated *acceptable* (Rom. 12:1, of the body which is holy, and 12:2, of God's will, and Eph. 5:10, of the kind of life which proves something to others) and *well-pleasing* (Phil. 4:18, of the Philippians' gift to Paul, and Heb. 13:21, of our works in God's sight). In all these cases, it refers to our works.
> >
> > (d) The context graphically describes Paul's labors for the Lord (chapter 4, and 5:11-15, 20), but leaves no hint of the uncertainty of salvation nor of salvation

by works. Rather, 5:19 shows that God reconciled us to Himself in Christ, and :21 describes our position as one of the righteousness of God in Christ.

Conclusion: verse 9 does not teach that our works will determine whether God receives us into heaven, but rather that we must strive to have our works acceptable or well-pleasing to Him when we appear before His judgment seat. The parallel reference to verse 10, I Corinthians 3:12-15, shows that even the Christian whose works are rejected will be saved. Therefore, there is no question of salvation here.

    (3) Problem #3: what does verse 10 mean by *receiving bad things?* Solution:

        (a) Obvious teachings: we will receive things done in the body. Some may be good, some, bad.

        (b) Parallels: Matthew 16:27 shows that we will receive according to our works. Therefore *receiving the things done* means receiving according to them. Compare Colossians 3:25 and Revelation 2:23. I Corinthians 4:5 indicates that God will consider the *counsels of the hearts* in evaluating our works. I Corinthians 3:12-15 and II John 8 reveal that the disobedient Christian will lose the reward he could have had.

        (c) Definitions: *receive* is #2865 in Strong. It is used in Hebrew 10:36, where to *receive the promise* obviously means to receive the fulfillment of the promise. Therefore, it can mean to receive one thing for another, or to receive a thing because of something else. *Bad* is #2556 in Strong. Matthew 24:48 translates it *evil*, describing one who beats others and is a drunkard; Mark 7:21 uses it of evil thoughts; Colossians 3:5, of evil concupiscence or desire; James 3:8 of the unruly tongue; Romans 14:20, of the result of doing something doubtful. Acts 16:28 translated it *harm*, referring to the result of a self-inflicted wound. Romans 13:10 renders it *ill*, describing the result of one man's actions upon another.

Conclusion: verse 10 teaches that bad things, whether acts or thoughts, will have definite results at the judgment seat of Christ. These results are shown in I Corinthians 3:12-15 to be the loss of the reward which could have been received.

4. Writing in my own words:

(1) For we know that if our earthly body were dissolved, we have a heavenly body created by God, not made with human hands, eternal in the heavens.

(2) In this earthly body we groan, earnestly desiring to be living in the heavenly body.

(3) But not being naked, without the fine linen which will represent our righteousness.

(4) For we that are in this earthly body do groan, being burdened, not desiring that we merely become spirits without bodies, but that we might have the heavenly body, that the possibility of death might be removed forever.

(5) For God has created us for this very purpose, and has also given us the Spirit as His guarantee.

(6) Therefore, we are always confident, knowing that while we are at home in this body, we are absent, physically, from the Lord.

(7) (For we walk by faith, not by sight)

(8) I repeat, we are confident and willing rather to be absent from this body and to be present with the Lord.

(9) Wherefore, we studiously strive to have our works acceptable to Him, both on earth and in heaven.

(10) For we must all appear before the judgment seat of Christ, that we may receive for the things which we did in the body, whether they were good or bad.

5. Writing the passage in the first person:

(1) For I know that if my earthly house of this tabernacle were dissolved, I have a building of God, an house not made with hands, eternal in the heavens.

(2) For in this I groan, earnestly desiring to be clothed upon with my house which is from heaven:

(3) If so be that being clothed I shall not be found naked.

(4) For I that am in this tabernacle do groan, being burdened: not for that I would be unclothed, but clothed upon, that mortality might be swallowed up in life.

(5) Now he that hath wrought me for the selfsame thing is God, who also hath given

41

unto me the earnest of the Spirit.

(6) Therefore I am always confident, knowing that, whilst I am at home in the body, I am absent from the Lord:

(7) (For I walk by faith, not by sight:)

(8) I am confident, I say, and willing rather to be absent from the body, and to be present with the Lord.

(9) Wherefore I labour, that, whether present or absent, I may be accepted of him.

(10) For I must appear before the judgment seat of Christ; that I may receive the things done in my body, according to that I have done, whether it be good or bad.

6. The verse to be memorized could be seven or ten.

Chapter 6

How To Study By Meditation

Scripture says much about meditation in the Word. Psalm 1:2 describes the blessed man as one who meditates in it day and night.

One of the most profitable ways to study the Bible is to take one verse and meditate on it only, writing down every thought that comes to mind from it. The following suggestions should prove to be helpful.

1. Write every thought, even the most obvious. Do not omit something because you think it is too simple. The obvious teachings of a verse will often lay the foundation for solving problems which may arise later. Also, what may be obvious to you may be unknown to another who is less experienced in the Christian life, and you should not overlook that which may help others.

2. Confine your thoughts to the particular verse you are studying. You will probably be reminded of other verses, but it is important to discipline yourself to stay with one at the time.

3. If the verse stirs your interest in a theme or topic elsewhere in scripture, make a note of that on a separate sheet of paper for further study. The same would be true of researching the Greek or Hebrew word, etc. Consult commentaries, word studies, and other helps only after you have written every possible conclusion from your meditation of the verse.

4. Try to forget pre-conceived ideas about what the verse means. Let the scripture speak to you, not vice versa.

5.   Make sure that your thoughts and conclusions do not contradict the general message of the whole Bible. Remember that God is unchangeable*(Mal. 3:6) and that His Word cannot contradict itself (Gal. 3:17).

6.   Do this over an extended period of time. Very often, our experiences will help us understand more about a verse, especially if we are obeying its teachings. Hebrews 5:14 teaches that our use of scripture will enable us to discern the proper meaning and application of it.

7.   The preacher or teacher could organize their conclusions into an outline which would be suitable for a sermon or lesson. The example which follows may be helpful in understanding more about this.

EXAMPLE OF THE MEDITATION METHOD

Psalm 119:71, *It is good for me that I have been afflicted; that I might learn thy statutes.*

1. This is primarily for a Christian, since *me . . . I* refers to David, who was certainly a believer.

2. Affliction is good for a believer.

3.   Affliction enables the believer to learn God's Word.

4.   There must be things in scripture that I could not learn without being afflicted.

5.   This learning must be experiential, since anyone can intellectually memorize scripture and understand at least some of its teachings.

6.   This learning must also be deeper than the most obvious teachings of scripture, since any Christian can

44

read the Bible and see what it teaches on the surface, without suffering affliction.

7. God can take unpleasant experiences, such as affliction, and bring good from them.

8. God either originated or permitted the afflictions, since the purpose of them is that I might learn His Word. Neither Satan, the world, or the flesh could have this purpose.

9. God's statutes are practical and should be applied to everyday experiences, including affliction.

10. His use of the word *thy* shows he is speaking to the Lord, therefore, in communion with Him.

11. Since the preceding is true, this is the reaction of a surrendered believer. Only that kind of Christian could view affliction in this way.

After reviewing these conclusions, one can easily see that they fall into three categories: #1, 10, and 11 speak of the person who has been afflicted; #2, 3, 4, 7, and 8 refer to the affliction; #5, 6, and 9 have to do with the learning. Therefore, an outline for use in preaching or teaching would look like this:

1.   THE PERSON WHO IS AFFLICTED

    A. . . . is a Christian, since *me* . . . I refers to David.

    B. . . . is in communion with the Lord, as seen by the word, *thy*.

    C. . . . is surrendered. Only this kind of believer could react in this manner.

2. THE AFFLICTION

   A.. . . is good for a believer.

   B.. . . enables the believer to learn God's Word.

   C.. . . will teach him things that he could not learn otherwise.

   D.God can take unpleasant experiences, such as affliction, and bring good from them.

   E.. . . is either originated or permitted by God, since the purpose of them is that we might learn His Word. Neither Satan, the world, or the flesh could have this purpose.

3. THE LEARNING

   A. . . . must be experiential, since anyone could intellectually memorize scripture and understand at least some of its teachings.

   B.. . . must be deeper than the most obvious teachings of scripture since any Christian can read the Bible and see what it teaches on the surface, without suffering affliction.

   C.God's statutes are practical and should be applied to everyday experiences, including affliction.

Chapter 7

How To Study A Parable

Since there is wide disagreement about the definition of a parable, as well as the importance of its details, it would be wise to consider a few facts regarding parables in general, before giving instructions about how to study them.

A parable is basically a comparison. Consider Mark 4:30, *And he said, Whereunto shall we liken the kingdom of God? or with what comparison shall we compare it?* The word *comparison* is from the Greek word *parabole* (usually translated parable), and *compare* is from the corresponding verb *paraballo*. Also, Christ prefaced many parables with the statement, *The kingdom of heaven is likened unto . . .* (Mt. 13:24, 35 al). A third proof is that several Old Testament scriptures, which are called parables, show the prophet comparing things or truths:

Numbers 23:18-24, Israel compared to a unicorn and lion;

Psalm 49:4, 12, 20, man compared to beasts that perish;

Ezekiel 17:2, 12, the king of Babylon to an eagle;

Ezekiel 20:45-49. God's judgment of Israel to a fire;

Ezekiel 24:3 ff, Jerusalem to a pot of boiling water;

Isaiah 46:5, where the Hebrew word which is translated *compare* is the same as that translated *parable* in Psalm 49:12, 20.

Parables are not fictitious, as many believe them to be. Hebrews 9:9 calls the tabernacle and its ordinances *a figure*, which is from the Greek word *parabole*. Hebrews 11:19 calls the sacrifice of Isaac a figure, from the same Greek word. Both these instances are historical and actual, not fictitious in the slightest. Also, Luke 12:16-20 gives the parable of the rich fool, but the major point of it is that, in the parable, God came to him and called him a fool because he had not prepared for eternity; God is certainly not a fictitious character! A third proof is that the utterances of Balaam are called parables (num. 23:7, 18; 24:3, 15, 20, 21, 23), but they can not be considered fiction since they came from God (Num 23:5). They are obviously statements of doctrine and prophecy, but they are not stories and certainly not fiction.

A parable can be a story, such as that of the lost son, recorded in Luke 15. However, in the light of the foregoing paragraph, such stories would have to be considered as true ones.

Sometimes the parable is given in the form of a proverb. The Hebrew word, which is translated *parable* 18 times, is translated *proverb* 19 times. That this is the equivalent of the New Testament word is seen by the fact that Matthew 13:35 says Christ fulfilled Psalm 78:2 when He taught in parables. Also, the Greek word *parabole* is translated *proverb* in Luke 4:23. New Testament examples of a parable in the form of a proverb are Luke 6:39 and Mark 3:23-27.

Occasionally, an institution or an experience is called a parable, as already noted in the references to Hebrews 9:9 (the tabernacle) and 11:19 (the sacrifice of Isaac).

Parables are designed to teach doctrine, a fact that is often denied. However, all of Balaam's utterances, called parables, definitely teach doctrine (see the third paragraph in this chapter). Also Psalm 78:2-4 shows that the purpose of Old Testament parables was to teach children the truth about God. And, Matthew 15:10-11 definitely teaches the doctrine of the depravity of the human heart, yet is called a parable in verse 15. The parallel passage, Mark 7:14:23, gives even more. Other examples are Mark 4:21-22, 33-34; Luke 8:16 and 11:33.

Based on these facts, a definition of a parable is submitted: a parable is a comparison between material and spiritual truth, designed to teach doctrine and obedience. It may be given in the form of a narrative, a proverb, or a reference to an event or institution.

We may rightly interpret the parables found in scripture by following these suggestions:

1. Determine the main lesson of the parable. Sometimes it is clearly stated at the beginning or ending, such as in Luke 18:1, 9 and 7:41-42, 47. At other times, it must be discerned from careful study, considering the context, especially the kind of people to whom the Lord spoke it.

2. Find the meaning of every detail of the parable by comparing scripture with scripture, as I Corinthians 2:13 evidently means. Remember that the basic meaning of the word is a comparison. The fact that the details are important and must be understood if we get the correct meaning is seen in Christ's explanation of the details of the first two parables in Matthew 13 (see verses 18-23 and 37-43); also, in Matthew 15:17-20

He explained the details of the parable He had told in verses 10-11. And if we remember that man is to live by *every word that proceedeth out of the mouth of God* (Mt. 4:4), we will realize that we must give attention to every word of Christ's parables.

The important thing to remember is that the symbolic meaning of a detail will be understood by parallel scripture. We must not resort to imagination, nor even to what may seem reasonable to us. Also, we must remember to make the details amplify and explain the main lesson, as Christ did in His explanations.

Finally, after the main lesson and symbolic meaning of details are learned, applications may be made to our present situation. See the example which follows.

EXAMPLE OF STUDYING PARABLES—

MATTHEW 13:44

1. The main lesson has been learned from a study of the details (next paragraphs) and a consideration of the fact that all the parables in this chapter are describing this present age when Satan is active (see verses 19,39). It is: Christ's purchase of the world and His preservation of Israel throughout the age, in spite of their rejection of Him.

2. Details:

> (a) The treasure represents Israel. In Exodus 19:5, God says, regarding Israel, *Now therefore, if ye will obey my voice indeed, and keep my covenant, then ye shall be a peculiar treasure unto me above all people: for all the earth is mine.* In spite of the fact that Israel did not meet God's conditions which were

laid down in this verse, Psalm 135:4 records the fact that, more than four hundred years later, God in grace still says, *For the Lord hath chosen Jacob unto himself, and Israel for his peculiar treasure.*

(b) The field represents the world, as Christ explained when He gave the meaning of the details of the wheat and tares (see verse 38).

(c) The man's hiding of the treasure pictures God's preservation of Israel, a fact which is miraculous in itself. Even unbelievers have recognized the unique situation regarding Israel. Never before has a race of people been scattered throughout the world, yet remained distinct in their ways of life. Even though Orientals and Negroes live in many nations different from their original home, they have been absorbed into the community and have adopted the customs and religions of their adopted nations, as well as the language. The Jews, on the contrary, have maintained their religion, customs, and language, as well as their love for their homeland. And our generation has been privileged to see the fulfillment of prophecy in their return and repossession of their land against tremendous obstacles and opposition from most of the world. All this is in fulfillment of such passages as Amos 9:8-9; Ezekiel 36:24; and Ezekiel 37.

(d) The man's joy is connected with his selling all that he had and buying that field. We are told in I Corinthians 6:19 that we are bought with a price; I Peter 1:18-19 specifies that price:

the precious blood of Christ. It was on the cross, then, that the Son of man made His purchase. I John 2:2 clearly states that He was the propitiation for the sins of the whole world; He did, indeed, buy the field!

However, one of the most amazing verses in the Bible concerning the cross is found in Hebrews 12:2, where we read that Christ endured the cross *for the joy that was set before him.* No doubt, the joy which He was that which He would experience as He redeemed mankind and satisfied God forever regarding their sins (Isa. 53:11). How great is His love! How incomprehensible that He could love sinners who reject Him and resist His attempts to call them to Himself! How we should thank God for this everlasting love (Jer. 31:3) and remember that His love to us is just as undeserved as His love for Israel.

    (e) When the Lord Jesus sold all that he had, He did indeed give up all that was precious to Him; He was forsaken by His friends (Mt. 26:31); He surrendered His holiness and *was made sin for us* (II Cor. 5:21); but, most of all, His fellowship with the Father was broken for the first time in all eternity, so that He cried, *My God, my God, why hast thou forsaken me?* (Mt. 27:46). Perhaps in heaven we will truly learn the depths of the price He paid for our redemption.

Chapter 8

How To Study People

1. Distinguish between various people with the same name. There are many Simons, Marys, etc. The Daniel who was thrown into the den of lions was not the same as the son of David (I Chron. 3:1), since they lived about 400 years apart!

2. Try to determine all of the person's names. Peter is also called Simon, Cephas, and Simeon. By comparing the three lists of the twelve disciples, we learn that two of them had multiple names: Judas Lebbaeus Thaddeus and Simon Zelotes, the Canaanite. We may learn all of a person's names by using the parallel references in the scripture or in the Treasury Of Scripture Knowledge, and by referring to a Bible dictionary or encyclopedia.

3. Determine the meaning of the character's name, names, or titles, using Strong's or Young's Concordance and a Bible dictionary or encyclopedia. Sometimes the scripture will give the key, as in Genesis 29:32-35; 30:6, 13, 20, 24. Compare Hebrews 7:2.

4. Collect all the scriptures which mention the person, using a concordance, Bible dictionary, or encyclopedia.

5. List the important people who had a significant influence on this person, giving references.

6. List the person's character traits, both good (honesty, persistence) and bad (selfishness, unreliability) and the causes of them, if known.

7. List the person's successes, both spiritually and otherwise, and give the reasons, if known.

8. List the person's failures, if any, and the causes.

9. Note whether this one is a type of Christ, and in what ways. For example, Deuteronomy 18:18 shows Moses to be a type of Christ. Take care not to make strained comparisons. Use scripture to show the similarities, and keep in mind the suggestions given in the chapter of this book on types. The benefit of this is to remind all of us that there are ways in which we can be like Christ.

10. Determine whether this person had a significant influence on another important person, or on a group of persons, such as a city or a nation. This influence could be good or bad.

11. List all spiritual crises in the character's life, such as conversion, call to the ministry, fall and restoration, vision of God, etc., and what might have caused them.

12. Note the obstacles which the person overcame, and how it was done.

13. Give the person a fitting title. Examples: Abraham was *the friend of God* (Jas. 2:23); David was *the sweet psalmist of Israel* (II Sam. 23:1). If there is a title in scripture, use it. Otherwise, make up one of your own.

EXAMPLE OF STUDYING PEOPLE: BARNABAS

1. Only one person in scripture is called Barnabas.

2. He was called Joses, by his parents, but was surnamed Barnabas by the apostles.

3. Joses may have been the Greek equivalent of the Hebrew name Joseph, which meant *adding,* according to Genesis 30:24. Barnabas means *the son of consolation,* according to Acts 4:36. It would help to remember that the word *consolation* had a broader meaning when the King James Version was translated: the Greek word is also translated *comfort* (Rom. 15:4), *exhortation* (Acts 13:15), and *intreaty* (II Cor. 8:4), so it means to encourage and plead with.

4. All the scriptures which mention him: Acts 4:36; 9:27; 11:22, 25, 30; 12:25; 13:1, 2, 7, 43, 46, 50, 14:12, 14, 20; 15:2, 12, 22, 25, 35, 36, 37, 39; I Cor. 9:6; Gal 2:1, 9, 13; Col. 4:10.

5. Those who significantly influenced him:

>   (1) The apostles, who surnamed him (Acts 4:36). He was, from that point on, known by that name only.
>
>   (2) The church at Jerusalem, which sent him to Antioch (Acts 11:22), from which the Holy Spirit sent him into missions.
>
>   (3) The representatives of James, negatively (Gal. 2:12-13).

6. Character traits:

>   (1) Unselfish (Acts 4:36-37; 14:13-15; 15:26).
>
>   (2) Considerate of those who are rejected by others (Acts 9:27).
>
>   (3) Encouraged new Christians (Acts 9:27; 11:23, 25-26; 14:21-23).
>
>   (4) Trustworthy, being sent by the Jerusalem church to learn the situation in Antioch (Acts 11:22). Compare 11:29-30; 12:25; and 15:2, 22.

(5) Spiritually perceptive, being able to discern the grace of God in the lives of the Christians at Antioch (Acts 11:22).

(6) A good man (Acts 11:24).

(7) Full of the Holy Spirit (Acts 11:24).

(8) Full of faith (Acts 11:24).

(9) A soul-winner (Acts 11:24).

(10) Faithful (Acts 11:26, *a whole year*; 15:2).

(11) A teacher (Acts 11:26; 13:1, and, possibly, a prophet)

(12) Spiritual (Acts 13:2).

(13) Bold (Acts 13:46).

(14) Persuasive (Acts 14:1).

(15) Impressive in appearance, because he was called Jupiter (Acts 14:12).

(16) Sensed his accountability to the church (Acts 14:27; 15:12).

(17) Determined; not easily swayed (Acts 15:37-39).

(18) Weak, at least on one occasion (Gal. 2:13, where *dissimulation* means hypocrisy. The Greek word is so translated in Mt. 23:28, and other places.)

7. Successes:

(1) He had probably succeeded in business, since he was a land owner (Acts 4:37).

(2) Convinced the apostles of Paul's genuineness (Acts 9;27).

(3) With Paul, taught the believers at Antioch to live such a life for Christ that the heathen recognized it (Acts 11:26). Also, in establishing many churches on their

missionary journeys.

(4) Persuaded Mark to resume Christian service, even after he had failed the Lord by forsaking missionary work (Acts 13:13; 15:38-39). Evidently, he was successful, because of Paul's favorable references to John Mark in Colossians 4:10 and II Timothy 4:11.

8. Failures: only one is recorded (unless the argument with Paul, in Acts 15:36-39, be considered such): the situation in Antioch, when he joined with the hypocrisy of Peter and others by refusing to eat with the Gentile Christians (Gal. 2:12-13). No reason for this failure is specified; we can only infer that, for some reason, he feared the opinion of the representatives of James. This was certainly the opposite reaction he had demonstrated at other times (Acts 13:46 and 15:2).

9. He was not a type of Christ.

10. He significantly influenced:

(1) The apostles, when he convinced them to receive Paul (Acts 9:27).

(2) Paul (Acts 9:27, implied), (Acts 11:25-26), persuading him to come with him to Antioch, from which the Holy Spirit sent him into missionary work.

(3) With Paul, the church at Antioch (Acts 11:26).

(4) The Jerusalem church (Acts 11:22; 15:25).

(5) John Mark, his nephew (Col 4:10), to travel with him and Paul in the ministry (Acts 12:25; 13:5); later, with himself alone

(15:39). Interestingly, the two men, which he influenced the most, wrote over half of the New Testament!

11. Crises:

(1) His conversion is not recorded.

(2) Selling his land and giving the money away (Acts 4:36).

(3) His call into missionary work (Acts 13:1-4).

(4) The argument with Paul (Acts 15:39), caused probably because he was so intent on getting John Mark back into Christian service.

(5) The controversy at Antioch over eating with Gentile believers (Gal. 2:12-13). See point 8, the failures.

12. Obstacles overcome:

(1) The hesitancy of the apostles to receive Paul. He overcame this by declaring Paul's conversion and preaching. Evidently, he did some research (Acts 9:27).

(2) The opposition of the "Pharisee-believers" (Acts 15:1-5). He and Paul overcame this by consistently testifying about what God had wrought in saving the Gentiles apart from circumcision.

(3) With Paul, he overcame much opposition in their missionary journeys by being faithful.

13. Title: the son of consolation (Acts 4:36), or, the encourager, or, the unsung hero of the New Testament.

Chapter 9

How To Study For Sermons

The preacher who would obey the command of II Timothy 4:2, *Preach the word*, must try to develop a homiletical mind which finds his sermon topics and outlines in the scriptures. While men differ according to their particular God-given style of preaching, certain guidelines are helpful to all.

An outline for one or more messages may be found by looking for repeated phrases in a chapter or book of the bible, such as:

> *(1) Yet ye say, Wherein* . . . Malachi 1:2, 6, 7; 2:14, 17; 3:7, 8, 13.
>
> *(2) Woe unto you, scribes and Pharisees, hypocrites!* Matthew 23:13, 14, 15, 23, 25, 27, 29. Note also, *ye blind guides*, verses 16, 17, 19, 24, 26.
>
> *(3) He that hath an ear, let him hear what the Spirit saith unto the churches*, Revelation 2:7, 11, 17, 29; 3:6, 13, 22.
>
> *(4) To him that overcometh*, Revelation 2:7, 11, 17, 26; 3:5, 12, 21.
>
> *(5) Trust in the Lord* . . . *Delight thyself* . . . *Commit thy way* . . . *Rest* . . . , Psalm 37:3-7.

Another enlightening thing to do is to consider the order in which words or phrases are found:

> (1) Grace and peace are always in that order, in Paul's salutations which open his epistles. Therefore, we learn that grace produces peace and peace is a result of grace.

Compare Ephesians 2:8 and Romans 5:1, for instance. Look up other verses about grace and peace, to see their relationship.

(2) The three phrases in Philippians 3:10. *The power of his resurrection* is victory over sin (Rom. 6:9-10), which is certainly required before we can know *the fellowship of his sufferings* and what it means to be *conformable unto his death.*

(3) Mark 7:6-13 reveals four downward steps that led the Pharisees to *making the word of God of none effect.* These steps are progressive, beginning with the heart attitude (:6) and proceeding through verses 7,8, and 9, with the tragic result described in verse 13.

(4) Psalm 84:11 shows that the Lord must be our sun before He can be our shield; we must have His light before we can expect Him to protect us. Also, we must have His grace before we can experience His glory.

(5) Hebrews 7:2 emphasizes order when it says that Melchisedec was first, King of righteousness and after that, King of peace. Righteousness is thus shown to come before peace. We must have the righteousness of God before we can be at peace with Him.

(6) See also James 3:17, where order is important: *the wisdom that is from above is first pure, then peaceable . . .*

It is also helpful to look for the various ways that a person or thing is described, either in a chapter, or in the overall context of the scripture:

(1) Acts 15 refers to becoming a Christian as being saved (:1), conversion (:3), hearing the word of the gospel and believing (:7); see also verses 9, 11, 14, 17, 18 and 19, for other descriptions.

(2) Psalm 59 refers to God in seven ways; see verses 1, 3, 5, 10, 11, 13, and 17.

(3) Hell is described in various scriptures as fire, a furnace of fire, a lake of fire, fire and brimstone, outer darkness, the second death, and the wine of the wrath of God.

(4) I Timothy 2:1 uses four words to refer to calling upon God.

(5) Christ has many names and titles throughout scripture: the seed of the woman, Shiloh, etc.

Repeated reading of a chapter will show several categories of thought:

(1) Philippians 3:4-9 describes Paul's past, while verses 10-19 speak of his present and verses 20-21 tell of his future.

(2) The work of each Person of the Trinity in providing our salvation is seen in Ephesians 2. Verses 1-10 tell of the Father, verses 11-18a refer to the Son, and 18b-22 describe the work of the Spirit.

Looking for "cause and effect," passages can be very beneficial:

(1) II Peter 1:5-7 lists seven things which should be added to the believer's faith; verse 8 gives the result if you do, while verse 9 shows the opposite, and verses 10-11 summarize the situation.

(2) The cause and effect relationship is obvious in II Timothy 2:11-13. Compare also Romans 10:9, 13, etc.

As we read a command or exhortation, we might ask, "How can this be done?" For instance how may we obey James 4:8, *Draw nigh to God . . .*"? Then, by looking up the key word, *draw nigh*, and various synonyms, we would find scriptures which give the answers:

(1) Hebrews 7:19 says that we draw nigh to Him by the *better hope* which He brought in by Christ, who is a better priest (see the context). In other words, we draw nigh to God by being saved through our Lord Jesus Christ. This would be parallel to Ephesians 2:13, *But now in Christ Jesus ye who sometimes were far off and made nigh by the blood of Christ.*

(2) Then, the Christian can *draw near with a true heart in full assurance of faith*, if our hearts are sprinkled from an evil conscience and our bodies are washed with pure water.

(3) Malachi 3:7 and context shows that they had gone away from God by disobedience to His ordinances; thus, to draw nigh, or return to Him, would be accomplished by obedience to those commands.

(4) Genesis 18:23 shows that Abraham drew near to God by interceding for Lot.

(5) Then, we are cautioned in Matthew 15:7-9 not to draw nigh to God in a hypocritical manner. It must be, not only from the lips, but from the heart also.

These are only a few suggestions about how to look for sermons as you read God's Word. Of course, the other methods discussed in this book would also yield much sermon material. Once a preacher begins to think this way, he will become more and more perceptive to thoughts, outlines, and questions, which will lead him to more material than he could exhaust!

Chapter 10

How To Study A Topic

1.   Using a complete concordance, find all the scriptures which name your topic, remembering the following:

> (a) Consider possible synonyms. For instance, if you study prayer, you should remember "supplication, intercession, giving thanks, calling upon God, and beseeching God." A dictionary of synonyms, such as Roget's Thesaurus, would be helpful.
>
> (b) Consider other forms of the word or phrase. If you are studying prayer, remember the words "pray, praying, prayeth, prayers," as well as "call, intreat, beseech," etc.

Besides a concordance, other books which would be helpful in collecting all the pertinent scriptures on the subject are:

> (a) A topical Bible, such as Nave's
>
> (b) A topical book, such as "The New Topical Textbook"
>
> (c) Chain references in such Bibles as Scofield and Thompson
>
> (d) A Bible dictionary
>
> (e) A Bible encyclopedia
>
> (f) The Treasury Of Scripture Knowledge

2.   As you read each scripture, write a brief statement telling what it teaches about the subject. Confine your remark to your subject; do not try to explain the whole verse. For instance, Mark 11:25

teaches something about God as Father, mentions heaven, and refers to trespasses, but you would simply say, "When we pray, we should forgive." You may have to read the context before deciding what the verse teaches about the subject.

3.   Organize your statements under logical headings. For instance, you could put verses about kneeling in prayer, standing in prayer, or lying prostrate in prayer, all under the one heading "Postures in Prayer."

4. Note the key passage or passages, if possible.

5.   Note the outstanding personal example(s) of your subject.

6.   Form your own definition of the subject, based on what you have learned from scripture, remembering to keep it as simple as possible and trying to limit it to one sentence.

EXAMPLE OF THE TOPICAL METHOD: FASTING

1.   All forms of the word: fast, fasted, fastest, fasting, fastings. Synonyms: neither did eat nor drink.

2. All scripture references, with comments:

Exodus 34.28, Moses fasted 40 days and nights, did not eat or drink. Compare Deuteronomy 9:9, 18.

Judges 20:26, Israel fasted in the house of God because of defeat. Fasting is associated with weeping, offerings, and prayer.

I Samuel 7:6, Israel assembled, fasted with offerings and confession of sin.

I Samuel 31:13 , for 7 days; associated with the defeat of Saul and Israel's army. Compare II Samuel 1:12.

II Samuel 12:16, David fasted for his sick child.

II Samuel 12:22, associated with weeping.

I Kings 19:8 ff, Elijah fasted 40 days and nights; did not need food because of the angel's provision.

I Kings 21:27, Ahab fasted with sackcloth and torn clothes, after Elijah's prophecy of his death.

II Chronicles 20:3, public fasting was proclaimed because of enemy attack.

Ezra 8:21, Ezra proclaimed a fast, for the purpose of afflicting self and to seek God's direction.

Ezra 8:23, it was rewarded.

Nehemiah 1:4, associated with weeping and mourning and prayer; it was for several days; was because of the affliction and reproach of people and the city of Jerusalem.

Nehemiah 9:1, Israel assembled; with sackclothes and earth; with observance of the feast of tabernacles and separation from sin.

Esther 4:3, public, with mourning and weeping and sackcloth and ashes, because of Haman's law to destroy them.

Esther 4:16, 3 days, neither eating nor drinking, for success in Esther's request of the king for deliverance.

Esther 5, 7, rewarded.

Psalm 35:13, David humbled his soul with fasting; because of his friends' sickness; with sackcloth and prayer.

Psalm 69:10, David chastened his soul with fasting: with weeping.

Psalm 109:24, fasting weakened David physically.

Isaiah 58:3, hypocritical; Israel wondered why God did not reward them for it; for the purpose of afflicting the soul; they fasted and had pleasure and worked at the same time. Compare Zechariah 7:5.

Isaiah 58:4, they fasted for strife and debate, and to have prayers answered.

Isaiah 58:5, with sackcloth and ashes.

Isaiah 58:6-7, God's chosen fast: loose the bands of wickedness, undo heavy burdens, let the oppressed go free, break every yoke, feed the hungry, house the poor, clothe the naked, provide for families. Such would be rewarded (:8-14).

Jeremiah 14:12, with offerings and prayer; will be rejected by Jehovah because they did not repent.

Jeremiah 36:6, 9, a fasting day was scheduled.

Daniel 6:18, the Babylonian king fasted for Daniel, denied himself music and sleep.

Daniel 9:3, associated with prayer, supplications, sackcloth and ashes, to seek God about the future.

Joel 1:14, the people are commanded to schedule a fast so they can seek God because of impending judgment. Compare 2:15.

Joel 2:12, commanded by God; with weeping, mourning, and turning to God.

Johan 3:5, Ninevites proclaimed a fast because they believed God's Word from Jonah about judgment, and sought Him to avert it (:9). All, from the least to greatest, fasted, including the king and even the animals (:5-7); done with sackcloth, prayer (:8), and repentance (:8); they neither ate nor drank (:7), and were rewarded (:10).

Zechariah 8:19, scheduled times of public fasting.

Matthew 4:2, Jesus did, for 40 days and nights.

Matthew 6:16, hypocritical fastings: sad countenance, disfigured faces, for man's approval (their only reward).

Matthew 6:17, 18, should not be seen or known by man. Should be in secret, for God only. Such will be openly rewarded.

Matthew 9:14, disciples of John and of Pharisees fasted often; disciples of Jesus did not.

Matthew 9:15, the disciples of Jesus did not fast because He was with them. In His absence, they will. Cp. Mark 2:18-20 and Luke 5:33-35.

Matthew 15:32, the multitude fasted because all food had been consumed during the 3 days they were with Jesus. It was probably not planned. Mark 8;1-3.

Matthew 17:21, fasting is necessary with prayer, for casting out a certain kind of demon, which causes self-inflicted wounds. Cp, Mark 9:29.

Luke 2:37, Anna served God with fastings and prayers night and day in the temple.

Luke 18:12, Pharisee boasted of fasting twice each week, as he prayed in the temple.

Acts 9:9, Paul fasted three days, with prayer, compare :11. Waiting on God for instruction.

Acts 10:30, Cornelius, a lost Gentile, fasted and prayed. The angel said that God noted his prayers and alms, but made no mention of the fasting (:4, 31).

Acts 13:2, Prophets and teachers fasted and ministered to the Lord: the Holy Spirit spoke to them as they did so, and revealed His call of Barnabas and Saul.

Acts 13:3, they fasted and prayed and laid hands on Barnabas and Saul and sent them away. Obviously, seeking God's blessing on them.

Acts 14:23, Paul and Barnabas prayed and fasted as they ordained elders and commended them to the Lord.

Acts 27:9, a scheduled fast among the heathen, evidently at the end of the season of calm weather.

Acts 27:33, Heathen sailors and soldiers fasted fourteen days because of the storm.

I Corinthians 7:5, with self-denial and prayer.

II Corinthians 6:5, a known practice of God's ministers (cp. : 4).

II Corinthians 11:27, Paul fasted often; could have meant being deprived of food, because of the context. Is in a list of sufferings which proved that he was truly a minister of Christ.

3. Organized under systematic headings.

   (1). How It Was Done
       a. By not eating or drinking (Ex. 34:28; Est. 4:16; Jon. 3:7)
       b. Sometimes publicly (Jud. 20:26; I Sam. 7:6; II Chr. 20:3; Ezra 8:21; Neh. 9:1; Est. 4:3; Jer. 36:6, 9: Joel 1:14; 2:15; Zech. 8:19)
       c. With prayer (Dt. 9:18; Jud. 20:26; Neh. 1:4; Ps. 35:13; Jer. 14:12; Dan. 9:3; Jon. 3:8).
       d. With weeping (Jud. 20:26; II Sam. 12:22; Neh. 1:4; Est. 4:3; Ps. 69:10; Joel 2:12).

e. With offerings (Jud. 20:26; I Sam. 7:6; Jer. 14:12)

f. With confession of sin (I Sam. 7:6).

g. With sackcloth (I Ki. 21:27; Neh. 9:1; Est. 4:3; Ps. 35:15; Isa. 58:5; Dan. 9:3; Jon. 3:8).

h. With torn clothes (I Ki. 21:27).

i. With observance of a feast day (Neh. 9:1).

j. With repentance (Neh. 9:1; Joel 2:12; Jon. 3:8).

k. With denial of music and sleep (Dan. 6:15).

l. At ordination of missionaries and elders (Acts 13:3; 14:23).

(2). How Long It Lasted

a. Forty days and nights (Ex. 34:28; I Ki. 19:8; Mt. 4:2).

b. Seven days (I Sam 31:13).

c. Three days (Acts 9:9).

d. Several days (Neh. 1:4).

e. Long enough to cause weakness (Ps. 109:24).

(3). People Who Fasted

a. Moses (Ex. 34:28).

b. Nation of Israel (Jud. 20:26; et al).

c. David (II Sam. 12:16; Ps. 35:13; 69:10; 109:24).

d. Elijah (I Ki. 19:8).

e. Ahab (I Ki. 21:27).

f. Ezra (Ezra 8:21).

g. Nehemiah (Neh. 1:4).

h. Esther and Mordecai (Est. 4:3, 16).

i. Daniel (Dan. 9:3).

j. Babylonian king (Dan. 6:18).

k. Ninevites and their animals (Jon. 3:5-9).

l. Christ (Mt. 4:2).

m. Disciples of John the Baptist (Mt. 9:14).

n. Disciples of Pharisees (Mt. 9:14; Lk. 18:12).

o. Anna (Lk. 2:37).

p. Paul (Acts 9:9).

q. Cornelius (Acts 10:30).

r. Prophets and teachers in Antioch (Acts 13:1-2)

s. Heathen soldiers and sailors (Acts 27:33).

4. Why They Fasted

a. Defeat (Jud. 20:26; 1 Sam. 31:13; II Sam. 1:12; Neh. 1:4; Acts 27:33).

b. For the sick child (II Sam. 12:16; cp. Ps. 35:13).

c. Divinely provided food was sufficient (I Ki. 19:8)

d. Impending judgment (I Ki. 21:27, to seek God's mercy; Est. 4:3; Joel 1:14; Jon. 3:5, 9).

e. Enemy attack (II Chr. 20:3).

f. To afflict self (Ezra 8:21; Isa. 58:3).

g. To seek God's direction (Ezra 8:21; Dan. 9:3; Acts 9:9; 10:30).

h. For success (Est. 4:16; Acts 13:3).

i. To humble the soul (Ps. 35:13).

j. To chasten the soul (Ps. 69:10).

k. For a friend in trouble (Dan. 6:18).

l. No available food (Mt. 15:32; II Cor. 11:27).

m. To serve God (Lk. 2:37; Acts 13:2).

n. To give evidence of being God's servants (II Cor. 6:4-5).

o. Hypocritically (Isa. 58:3, 4, for strife and debate, enjoying pleasure; Zech 7:5; Jer. 14:12, would not repent; Mt. 6:16-17; Lk. 18:12).

(5). How God Rewarded It

a. By delaying judgment (I Ki. 21:27-29).

b. By providing protection (Ezra 8:23).

c. By giving favor with the king (Est. 4:16-5-3, ch.7).

d. By removing judgment (Jon. 3:10).

(6). How God Commands It To Be Done

a. By helping others in their needs (Isa. 58:6).

(1) Loose the bands of wickedness

(2) Undo heavy burdens

(3) Let the oppressed go free

(4) Break every yoke

(5) Feed the hungry

(6) House the poor

(7) Clothe the naked

(8) Hide not from our own flesh

b. In secret, anointing the head and washing the face so that others will not know (Mt. 6:16-18).

c. Along with denying ourselves the pleasures

72

of the physical _relationship between husband and wife (I Cor. 7:5), but only temporarily and with the other's consent.

d. With Prayer (I Cor. 7:5).

(7). Why We Should Fast

a. Christ said to do so (Mt. 9:14-15).

b. To cast out a certain kind of demon (Mt. 17:21).

c. Probably for the same reasons that the godly people did, in Bible days. See points 4a, b, d, e, f, g, h, i, j, m, and n.

d. Christ promised that it would be rewarded (Mt. 6:18).

4. The key passage is Matthew 6:16-18, Moreover when ye fast, be not, as the hypocrites, of a sad countenance: for they disfigure their faces, that they may appear unto men to fast. Verily I say unto you, They have their reward. But thou, when thou fastest, anoint thine head, and wash thy face; that thou appear not unto men to fast, but unto thy Father which is in secret: and thy Father, which seeth in secret, shall reward thee openly.

5. The outstanding personal example is the Lord Jesus Christ (Mt. 4:2). If He fasted, how much more should we?

6. A definition: fasting is self-denial, usually of food and drink, but could be of other things (Isa. 58:6-7 and I Cor. 7:5), which is done because the person senses a special need of God, either in his own life or in that of another.

Chapter 11

How To Study A Type

Even though types have been abused, we should not ignore them, because scripture clearly teaches that persons, things, and events were foreshadowings of greater persons and truths which would come in New Testament days. We may avoid foolishness and doctrinal error by learning these facts about types and following the suggestions about how to study them.

Fact #1: scripture teaches typology. Melchisedec was a type of Christ, *being made like unto the Son God* (Heb. 7:3). Adam was a figure of him that was to come (Rom. 5:14, where *figure* is from the Greek word *tupos*; see the next paragraph).

Fact #2: the word type is from the Greek word *tupos,* which is translated as follows:

> (1) Ensample, Philippians 3:17; II Thessalonians 3:9
>
> (2) Example, I Timothy 4:12
>
> (3) Fashion, Acts 7:44
>
> (4) Figure, Romans 5:14; Acts 7:43
>
> (5) Form, Romans 6:17
>
> (6) Manner, Acts 23:25
>
> (7) Pattern, Titus 2:7; Hebrews 8:5
>
> (8) Print, John 20:25. The obvious meaning of the word is that of an impression made on one thing by another. The *print of the nails* in the hands of Christ is a good example of this definition. We might also compare our modern use of the word "typewriter."

Fact #3: there are various classifications of types, such as:

    (1) Persons (Adam, Rom. 5:14)

    (2) Institutions (Marriage, Eph. 5:22-33)

    (3) Offices (Priesthood, Ps. 110:4 and Heb. 4:14 -16)

    (4) Events (Passover, I Cor. 5:7)

    (5) Things (Brazen serpent, Jn. 3:14)

The following suggestions for the study of types will be helpful in preventing one from foolish and unscriptural interpretations.

    (1) Use only a divinely-ordained person, thing, or incident, such as manna from heaven, or Moses' smiting of the rock. No ordinary event, such as the mere eating of food or putting on of apparel, would be a type. No New Testament scripture refers to a mundane, common event as a type.

    (2) Have a scripture which proves your comparison. Example: just as the manna came from heaven (Ex. 16:4), so Christ came from heaven (Jn. 6:33, 38). Thus, one would not make the error of "discovering a new doctrine."

    (3) If there is a New Testament passage which discusses the type in detail (more or less), be sure to consider that first, to avoid a wrong doctrinal slant. For example, Romans 5:12-21 for Adam; John 6:31-58 for the manna; Hebrews 9:1-28 for the tabernacle.

    (4) Note, not only the points of comparison,

but those of contrast, as well. After telling us that Adam is a type of Christ (Rom. 5:14), verses 15-17 show several contrasts.

(5)   Use your own knowledge of the New Testament, as you read repeatedly and meditate on the Old Testament passage. Note all comparisons and contrasts. Then, consult parallel references. As a last resort, read what others may have written, in commentaries and typical studies.

The reason for studying types is not to discover some new doctrine, or to appear to be novel, but to find *in all the scriptures the things concerning himself* (Jesus). It is to enable us to take His yoke upon us and learn of Him, increasing in the knowledge of God, thereby reaping the benefits described in such scriptures as Psalm 19:7-11 and Philippians 3:10-14.

EXAMPLE OF TYPOLOGY: ADAM

Adam was *the figure (tupos) of him that was to come* (Rom. 5:14). As such, several comparisons and contrasts are made in Romans 5:

(1) His act affected the world (:12). II Corinthians 5:19, *God was in Christ, reconciling the world unto himself.*

(2) The gift which came by Christ is much more than the penalty which came by Adam (:15).

(3) Adam's one sin brought judgment, but Christ brought justification for many offences (:16).

(4) By Adam's sin, death reigned over us; by Christ's grace and righteousness, we reign (:17).

(5) One act of both Adam and Christ was imputed

to all people (:17-18).

These comparisons and contrasts would naturally encourage us to seek others, from the Genesis record. First, the comparisons.

(1) A unique beginning: Adam, from the dust (Gen. 2:7); Christ, from the Holy Spirit through a virgin mother (Lk. 1:27, 35), humanly speaking, of course. As God, He had no beginning (Mic. 5:2).

(2) Adam was given dominion over all the earth (Gen. 1:26_28). Christ will have it when He returns (Isa. 9:6-7).

(3) Adam and his bride were to be fruitful (Gen. 1:28). Likewise, Christ and His bride (Rom. 7:4).

(4) Adam was to subdue all the earth (Gen. 1:28). Christ will do the same (I Cor. 15:24).

(5) God gave Adam work to do (Gen. 2:15). The Father sent Christ to do a specific job (Jn. 3:17).

(6) God commissioned Adam to *keep* the garden (Gen. 2:15). Christ kept all of those whom the Father gave Him (Jn. 17:12).

(7) God commanded Adam (Gen. 2:16). The Father obviously did likewise, to Christ, since He said *I do nothing of myself; but as my Father hath taught me, I speak these things* (Jn. 8:28).

(8) God made a wife for Adam (Gen. 2:18-25). Christ also has one wife, the church (Eph. 5:25-33).

(9) Adam was exceptionally wise, naming all the creatures (Gen. 2:19-20); Christ is more so (Col. 2:3).

(10) Adam was wounded so his bride could be formed (Gen. 2:21-22). Because of Christ's wounds (Isa. 53:5), we can become His bride.

(11) Adam's wife was deceived into sin (I Tim. 2:14). Likewise, Christ's bride had a deceitful heart (Jer. 17:9).

(12) Adam evidently sinned deliberately, according to the implication in I Timothy 2:14. Christ deliberately took upon Himself our sins (I Pet. 2:24).

(13) It was because of the woman that Adam sinned (Gen. 3:6). It was because of us that Christ became sin (II Cor. 5:21).

(14) Adam's sin brought sorrow to him (Gen. 3:17). Because He took our sins, Christ was a man of sorrows (Isa. 53:3).

(15) Adam's sins resulted in separation from God (Gen. 3:23-24). When He became sin for us, there was a separation between the Son and the Father (Mt. 27:46).

(16) Adam's name was given to his wife (Gen. 5:2), so, Christ's name has been given to us (I Pet. 4:16).

(17) Adam's likeness was imparted to his son (Gen. 5:30); so, believers will be conformed to the image of Christ (Rom. 8:29).

Now, the contrasts.

(1) Adam had the image of God (Gen. 1:26-27), but all the fullness of the Godhead dwelled in Christ, bodily (Col. 2:9).

(2) Adam came to a paradise, an earth without sin (Gen. 2:8). Christ came to an exceedingly sinful earth.

(3) While Adam was asleep, his bride was formed (Gen. 2:21-22). The Lamb's bride was formed by His death (Eph. 5:25).

(4) After his sin, Adam hid from God (Gen. 3:8). After He became sin, Christ presented Himself to God (Heb. 9:12-14).

(5) Adam blamed Eve for his sin (Gen. 3:12), but Christ *his own self* took our sins upon his body on the cross (I Pet. 2:24).

(6) Adam's sin brought a curse to the ground (Gen. 3:17). Christ's sacrifice for sin made it possible for the curse to be removed (Isa. 35).

(7) An innocent animal had to be slain for Adam (implied in the *coats of skins*, Gen. 3:21), but Christ became the innocent Lamb of God for us (II Cor. 5:21).

(8) Adam's life ended (Gen. 5:5) but Christ lives forever (Rev. 1:18).

Chapter 12

How To Study A Word

1. After choosing the English word, determine the Greek or Hebrew word from which it has been translated by using a Strong's or Young's Concordance. Be sure to look up all forms of the English word.

2. List all the English words by which that Greek or Hebrew word is translated, in scripture. Try to determine, from the context, why the translators might have chosen that particular word in preference to the other possibilities.

3. Form a definition, based on your findings from points 1 and 2.

4. List what the Bible teaches about the word, considering each verse where it is found, keeping in mind the most-frequently-asked questions about it. Remember that one fact may be taught in two or more places. List that fact only once, giving all the references which teach it. Look up each English word and the verse which has the particular number by it. See the example.

5. Try to form your list of information into an outline which might be used to teach others. Ability to do this will come from studying the outlines of other people and from practice.

6. List the major passage which deals with your word, or subject, if there is one.

EXAMPLE OF A WORD STUDY

1. English word: chastening. Various forms: chasten, chastened, chastenest, chasteneth, chastening, chastise, chastised, chastisement, chastiseth.

2. Using Strong's Concordance, all are from #3811, *paideuo*, translated *chasten, chastise, instruct, learn,* and *teach*; and from #3809, *paideia,* translated *chastening, chastisement, instruction,* and *nurture.* (Only the New Testament has been used, since several verses are common to both Old and New Testaments: Job 5:17; Prov. 3:11; and Heb. 12:5.) *Chasten* emphasizes the aspect of punishment. *Learn, teach, instruction, and nurture* show that the goal is not our suffering, but our learning.

Using Young's Concordance, we learn that the two Greek words are *paideuo* and *paideia.* Then, on page 82 of the Index-Lexicon To The New Testament in the rear of the book, we learn that *Paideia* is translated *chastening* 3 times, *chastisement* once, *instruction* once, and *nurture* once. *Paideuo* is translated *chasten* six times, *chastise* twice, *instruct* once, *teach* twice, *be learned* once, and *learn* once. Then it would be necessary to look up all these English words in the main body of the concordance, being sure to find them under the proper Greek heading.

3. A defnition: chastening is an act of God, whereby He uses various methods and experiences, some of which may be unpleasant, to teach or train us in His ways.

4. What the Bible teiaches about this word: Revelation 3:19, the Lord Jesus chastens all whom He loves. See also Hebrews 12:6.

I Corinthians 11:32, We are chastened of the Lord that we should not be condemned with the world.

II Corinthians 6:9, Paul was chastened.

Hebrews 12:10, earthly fathers chasten us for their pleasure, but God, for our profit.

Hebrews 12:7, it is an evidence of sonship. See also verse 8.

Hebrews 12:5, we are not to despise it. Also, it is compared to being rebuked.

Hebrews 12:6, it is compared to being scourged.

Hebrews 12:11, it is not pleasant but afterward it yields the peaceable fruit of righteousness.

Luke 23:16, 22, Pilate chastised Jesus.

II Timothy 2:25, the pastor is to instruct with meekness. *Instruct* is the same as *chasten*.

II Timothy 3:16, the scripture is profitable for instruction (chastening).

I Timothy 1:20, God uses Satan to teach people not to blaspheme.

Acts 7:22, Moses was learned (chastened) in all the wisdom of Egypt.

Ephesians 6;4, Parents are to teach, chasten, nurture, their children according to the Lord.

Titus 2:12, the grace of God teaches us to deny ungodliness, etc.

    5.   An outline which may be useful in teaching others:

        (1). Definition of chastening

           a. Instruction (II Tim. 3:16; Acts 7:22; 22:3; Eph. 6:4)

           b. Punishment (Lk. 23:16, 22; Heb. 12:5-11)

2. Kinds of chastening
   a. Punitive (David, II Sam. 12:10)
   b. Preventive (Paul, II Cor. 12:7)
   c. Educative (Job)
3. Methods of chastening
   a. Sickness and death (I Cor. 11:30, 32)
   b. Satan (I Tim. 1:20)
   c. Scripture (II Tim. 3:16)
   d. Grace (Titus 2:12)
4. Reasons for enduring chastening-Hebrews 12
   a. Because of the scriptural exhortation (:5. Verses 5-6 are from Prov. 3:11-12)
   b. Because it is an evidence of sonship (:6-8). Note: EVERY. George Henderson said, "God had one son without sin, but He never had a son without suffering."
   c. Because our heavenly Father is worthy of more reverence than earthly fathers (:9)
   d. Because it is for our profit (:10)
   e. Because it enables us to partake of His holiness (:10)
   f. Because it yields the peaceable fruit of righteousness (:11). Compare breaking ground, harrowing, planting, cultivating, reaping!
5. Attitudes in chastening
   a. Forgetting (:5). Hence, the need for 10:25. Compare II Peter 3:1.
   b. Despising (:5). George Henderson said, "They were judging God by the pressure of His hand, instead of by the Word of His lips."

c. Fainting (:5). Verse 3 is the cure.

d. Enduring (:7). Verse 7 states that sons endure; verse one exhorts us to run the race with endurance. Thus, we see again the theme of the epistle.

e. Being in subjection (:9)-allowing the chastening to have its designed results.

6. The major passage: Hebrews 12:5-11.

Chapter 13

Additional Suggestions

Set a definite time to do your Bible study: a particular day, a particular time, and a certain length of time. Use common sense about the length: do not try to study for two or three hours if you are beginning. Once the time has been established, let nothing interfere, short of emergencies or situations beyond your control.

Learn all you can by yourself, using your Bible and the basic tools suggested in this book, before reading commentaries.

Encourage another Christian to do a similar study at the same time, then compare your notes. We can all learn from each other. Several Christians who are serious about personal Bible study could form a study group and meet periodically to compare notes and discuss.

After completing two or three of these methods, you will find yourself "bursting with desire" to share what you have learned with others. Start doing so, on a one-to-one basis. This is one the greatest ways to witness. Then, seek an opportunity to teach a class, or to otherwise serve the Lord publicly.

If you do not understand something in this book, seek help from a more experienced Christian.

Read Proverbs 2:1-5 and follow its commands to seek God's wisdom as you would seek silver and hidden treasures; then, you will experience the fulfillment of the promise of verse 5!

Other Titles Available
from Bethel Baptist Print Ministry

ANDREW MURRAY BOOK TITLES - 25% discount to bookstores, churches, or to individuals ordering 5 or more copies of any one title.

- Abide in Christ (169 pages) .... $ 7.00
- Absolute Surrender (102 pages) .... $ 4.00
- Humility (68 pages) .... $ 4.00
- The Deeper Christian Life (72 pages) .... $ 4.00
- The Holiest of All (*Devotional Commentary on Hebrews*) (410 pages) $12.00
- The Master's Indwelling (122 pages) .... $ 5.00
- The Ministry of Intercession .... $ 7.00
- The New Life (204 pages) .... $ 7.00
- The Power of the Blood & the Blood of the Cross .... $ 9.00
- **The Prayer Life** .... $ 6.00
- The Prophet Priest (58 pages) .... $ 4.00
- The School of Obedience (84 pages) .... $ 4.00
- The Secret of Fellowship (73 pages) .... $ 4.00
- The Spirit of Christ (278 pages) .... $ 8.00
- The State of the Churches (113 pages) .... $ 5.00
- The True Vine (64 pages) .... $ 4.00
- With Christ in the School of Prayer (220 pages) .... $ 7.00

BRUCE LACKEY BOOK TITLES -

- Can You Trust Your Bible? (36 pages) .... $ 3.00
- Cremation, Divorce & Other Matters (61 pages) .... $ 4.00
- Jude, A Commentary and Self-Study (60 pages) .... $ 4.00
- God's Promise About Children (24 pages) .... $ 3.00
- 1 Peter: The True Grace of God (114 pages) .... $ 5.00
- Proverbs for the Family (88 pages) .... $ 4.00
- Repentance is More Than a Change of Mind (32 pages) .... $ 3.00
- 10 Ways to Study Your Bible (78 pages) .... $ 4.00
- What the Bible Teaches About Drinking Wine (19 pages) .... $ 2.00
- Why I Believe the Old King James Bible (88 pages) .... $ 4.00

DAVID CLOUD BOOK TITLES

- Avoiding The Snare of 7th Day Adventism (165 pages) .... $ 5.95
- Biblical Separation (72 pages) .... $ 3.00
- CCM Under the Spotlight (450 pages) .... $ 19.95
- Concise King James Bible Dictionary (90 pages) .... $ 4.95
- CD-ROM—Fundamental Baptist Library (100-meg, 80,000 pages) .... $ 89.95
- Darjeeling Disaster (The) (108 pages) .... $ 4.95
- Dynamic Equivalency (70 pages) .... $ 5.00
- Evangelicals & Rome (371 pages) .... $ 19.95
- Examining "The King James Only Controversy" (115 pages) ...... $ 4.95
- For Love of the Bible (460 pages) .... $ 29.95